Financial Planning: Where Did We Go Wrong?

George Burney

BK
ROYSTON
Publishing

Feb 20th
2024

To DOREEN
FINANCIAL
Freedom Comes
By The choices
we make For
our Future
GEORGE BURNEY

BK Royston Publishing
http://www.bkroystonpublishing.com
bkroystonpublishing@gmail.com

© 2024

Cover Design: Elite Cover Designs

ISBN-13: 978-1-959543-92-3

Printed in the United States of America

Disclaimer: The information in this book is not to be taken as financial advice, the book is for informational purposes only. Please consult a certified financial planning consultant for all of your financial goals. The author and BK Royston Publishing are not responsible for the contents that will be taken as financial advice.

Dedication

This book is in honor of and dedicated to my sister Julene Burney who passed away.

Acknowledgements

This book would not have been possible if we're not for Dr Julia Royston and the staff of Royston publishing, thank you Dr Royston for helping me fulfill my dreams. 6 years ago, on my birthday, I wanted to do something different so I asked Terri if she would help me take some food out to the homeless community? She was all in and then told me the story of how my mother-in-law would make lunch for the homeless community in California. My mother-in-law Naomi Davie was a dialysis patient for many years and was moved to help those in need. We originally named this "Lunch With Naomi." Inspired by her willingness to help others "Outreach Saturday" was born.

Today Outreach Saturday has fed over 10,000 people and also has sent out care packages to Melbourne Australia with hygiene kits to a nonprofit organization called "Christmas On The Streets." Roseanne Rafael she and her nonprofit feed thousands of people a week.

Outreach Saturday is on smaller scale as it's just Terri and I. We don't post our outreach online (Facebook or Instagram) mainly just through our phone contacts and other friends. Through this method, we found out people wanted to help us including a nonprofit that took us totally off guard. So, I want to acknowledge the following people who helped us
Raul and Deymi Campos, Kelsey Lee Hollenbeck and Tyler Hollenbeck, Dr Metta Sabins, Carol M, also Ileana Alverez. Also, to the nonprofit who donated to our cause Kimberly Allen, Gregory Allen Jr, Cathy Allen, Greg Allen Sr, Rhonda Irons, Mother Annie Sanders who is a member of Bethel Christian Church. These people together donated thousands of dollars and without their

support "Outreach Saturday" would not be here today.

We are so very grateful to them and their compassion to help others. Their only question was "how can I help?"

Table of Contents

Chapter 1

The Power Of Planning A Stable Financial Future

All right, let's get to work. When it comes to wealth and prosperity, we all might have been guilty of scrolling on YouTube or Instagram pages watching very slick editing of people in a Tesla, Mercedes driving into a seven-thousand square foot home, or maybe an entrepreneur dangling a carrot in front of you to click the link in the bio.

So, is it the flashy lifestyle, or maybe we want to live our older years without the burden of debt? Debt affects every area of your life, and it can also leave a burden on the next generation of family members who have no idea of what generational wealth is. The focus of this book is to get us to think about how we can live a better life without the worry of debt hanging over our families for decades and, in some cases, generations.

In planning for retirement, and even life, you must remember the goal is not to accumulate stuff and brand name items so that we can show it off or brag about our Louie Vuitton shades. While there is nothing wrong with having nice things, the focus has to be on family and community and how we leave a lasting legacy.

I think, at times, wealthy people get a bad rap because, in our view, or what we hear is that they pay no taxes and take away from the tiny business owners, and it goes on and on. So, here's the question you can ask yourself. Who were the first teachers who taught you about financial education? Mom? Dad? Your teachers? Grandmother? Who laid the groundwork for financial literacy in your life?

Looks can be so deceiving. Years ago, I heard a quote from Dr. Myles Monroe. He said, "God doesn't give you what you ask for. He gives you what you can manage."

Management is the next level after faith, because once you build wealth, the next level will be your management skills

The lack of knowledge and application will only prolong your agony, and the lack of planning will keep you from your dreams.

Most Americans are taught to go to school then work a job for two-thirds of their lives, collect a pension and retire, but little teaching goes into budgeting and savings and having written goals. So, what are your goals? Do you have a plan? A mentor? What will you do on your first day of retirement? Do you have enough to live on? And the list goes on and on.

Hopefully, this book will make you think and act, because if you don't have a plan for your life, some stranger will plan it for you.

I find it hard to believe that in public schools across the United States, grades 1 through 12, there is no financial literacy being taught. Why is that? So, our first education about money comes from our parents and grandparents.

I remember them as a young boy. I went on a field trip to Washington Mutual Savings bank. I believe I was ten years old. The president of the bank took our group on tour in the bank vault where they kept the cash and the safety deposit boxes, and a massive security guard was watching our every move. Still, you could tell by his demeanor that he was unhappy about thirty 10-year-olds running back and forth saying, "Money! Money, give us some money." Yes, you can include me in the group. I was saying it along with my classmates.

However, the reason I won't forget the field trip is that the bank president took us to the boardroom, and as she opened the door, my eyes glazed across the room in astonishment as I looked at a table that was as long as the state of California, with so many chairs and coffee pots everywhere.

So, the bank president asked, "Any questions?"

My hand flew up quickly and I said, "Yes, what goes on in here?"

The president replied, "This is where we decide the future of our customers."

I have never have forgotten that field trip.

I do realize that the wealthy people here in America get a share of criticism about how they got rich and the one percent of wealth holders across the world get raked over the coals as the middle-class demands they pay taxes. I do get it and understand the views of the middle class as they continue to live from paycheck to paycheck.

Consider this: could it be that the one percent of wealthy people were taught about financial education at an early age? Could it be that their parents had a plan in place for their future?

As you read this chapter, I would like you to be a critical thinker for the next few paragraphs. Not all wealthy people are greedy and hoard money for themselves, and not all rich people had their money given to them. It is our perception of how we view others. Social media has really, at times, unplugged our creative thinking process and has allowed us to see others in a different light.

What have Instagram, YouTube and Facebook done? Well, they have allowed some people to create a lifestyle that they don't live.

Those who know me know I drive a 2010 Honda Accord and live in a modest home which is just enough for Terri and me.

So, here's the problem that doesn't get a lot of likes or thumbs up. Why? Because it doesn't scream SUCCESS! By the way, I love my Honda.

In today's society, young people have great opportunities to make money and create wealth at a fast pace. It is almost making the college degree look obsolete as the younger generation is making strides very quickly.

However, this is a very important question. Do you have a financial plan? Make that two very important questions for you to answer. Who is going to teach you how to prepare for your future?

We have all heard the saying 'it's never too late'. However, that catchphrase needs to be put to bed because it doesn't work for the 21st century. Yes, we can indeed start over, but the question remains; do we use our time wisely? And meanwhile, the clock of middle age is vastly approaching.

The popular financial guru Dave Ramsey has been teaching people for years how to get out of debt and stay away from credit cards. He had people calling into his show with desperation in their voices because they realized they didn't plan for the future.

Now, this is the hard part to read. If you are over 65 and have no retirement, savings or 401k plan, it is possible that you may not reach your goal. That is because, once you reach a certain age, you have more years behind you than in front of you.

Where we lose our place in life is by going after material wealth like there's no tomorrow. So, to clarify, I am not against material wealth. It is okay to have nice things, but keep in mind that is what they are—things.

What the American family needs is the essentials in life for the future.

Okay, let's think this out. Some corporations will give raises to their employees, anywhere from one to three percent over three years, but in most metropolitan cities, the cost of living goes up six percent a year. It's like the hamster in the spinning wheel, going fast but not getting anywhere. So, how does one go about planning a stable financial future?

Well, adequate information and application are your most powerful tools. If you have spent any time on YouTube or Instagram, you know that entrepreneurs are everywhere, telling you how to get rich fast and in a hurry. However, keep in mind, you are only getting the edited version of their success. YouTube has become the new infomercial.

In financial planning, time is of the essence. You must have a budget, save your receipts and avoid using credit cards. Set a weekly goal of how much you want to save. Also, make the sacrifice of helping those who are in need.

Avoid pointing the finger at others, or being mad at rich people. Chances are they don't know you're mad at them; they are too busy building generational wealth.

Your plan must include a mentor who knows how to help you and your family.

This is what is lacking in most families—planning. Now, planning does not stop the storms from coming, but it does minimize the damage, because a rainy day is on the horizon. In 1995, my oldest brother passed away. My grandmother needed a new roof and a new furnace for her home. This happened all in one month, costing me over $13,000. Yes, life happens! It so happened that my J.I.C.—just in case—fund had $15,000 in it. So, what did I do?

I started to build it back up again. If we are honest with ourselves, we hate to see payday coming because most workers realize that after working for two weeks to get the check on Friday, by Monday, the check has gone to mortgage, utilities, WIFI bill, children's school supplies, and the list goes on. It's as if the wealth gap is getting wider. If you don't plan, there will be no tomorrow.

All right, another question for you: how many people do you know who are debt-free? I'll give you a few minutes to think it over. Debt-free, no mortgage, no credit card , no student loans. How many of your friends, family church members, coworkers? I guarantee you if you do know any debt-free people, chances are they planned for their future. Keep in mind, the goal is not to collect the most stuff. The goal is to retire (not from life) but from your job that, if you are honest, is not paying you enough. Money is a subject that others shy away from because they realize that their future is in the hands of someone else. Until you have the deed or title in your hand, the bank owns your home and your car. This book is a tool to make you rethink your position about planning your financials. You can be a family man with three kids or a single mom, someone is depending on you to make their life better. And when you plan, what you are doing is securing the future for the people you love. Time is so vital for financial planning, and doing it early in life will take pressure off your future. Not planning, will add another ten to twenty years to your job.

As I mentioned earlier about the old saying, 'it's never too late to start over again',

this is not true. You can wait too long, because time will catch up with you and your choices, and it's sad when your future catches up with you and you are not prepared for your tomorrow.

So, in your planning, you must have people who have your best interests at heart, those who are certified in their field as a financial planner, because you want your money to keep up with the cost of living when you decide to retire. You don't want to live from paycheck to paycheck when you retire; it will force you back in the workplace with no future. The main concern of the working man and woman is 'will I have enough to live off.' Do not put it off; plan for your tomorrow now. Your family is depending on you; don't let them down.

In the church world, there has always been an emphasis placed on seedtime and harvest.

While this is a mandate in the scriptures, we must remember that a harvest does not grow overnight. The field must be watered and the soil must be in the right climate for the crop to grow. Now, can there be a twenty-four hour turnaround on your giving? By all means, it can happen. It depends on your faith.

So, where did teachers and parents go wrong on financial planning?

Well, it could very well be that they were giving us information that was outdated, stats that were outdated and information that had holes in it, allowing us to believe that working on a job for forty years would bring about financial independence.

I am sure, by now, you realize that I'm not a financial planner. However, I do realize there are huge holes—I mean like Swiss cheese holes—between the wealthy and the poor.

If we are honest with ourselves, the middle class is no more. It's not that rich people are evil and are conspiring to take over the world. They have been taught the game, their teachings about wealth have been instilled in them from birth, it's all they know.

Their heirs will never have to work a day in their life. Why? Because their teachers taught them how to prepare for their future.

In preparation, you must learn to pivot, prepare and move. Don't let your emotions allow you to stand still, because if you do, you will be caught up in a storm of questions wondering if you did the right thing. Planning a budget is a key component on how to get ahead. You cannot buy everything you see, and there will be times you will have to say no to your friends who want to go out for dinner. Your children might have to go without that $300 or those $400 Jordans.

Uh, just a quick sidebar. Back in the day, my grandmother paid $12 for some Converse All-Stars, and she thought that was the worst thing ever. She said, "You too short to be getting some $12 tennis shoes, and you won't be getting any more!" Those were the days.

The frustration of planning for your future is not knowing how things work and who to go to when things are broken. And meanwhile, the clock is still moving and ticking.

Chapter 2

Build Wealth, Not Credit

We have always heard how important credit scores are, but they not a debt green light. Let's think this out. While having a high credit score is important, you must realize it only opens another door for you to borrow more money, which puts you in more debt. I am just guessing that airline miles won't make you a millionaire. In order for you to get a$1,000 back from Chase or Discover card, you have to spend $100,000. The math does not add up.

In the Old Testament, there's a powerful scripture that reminds us that 'the borrower is slave to the lender'. And when you borrow, you are on the hook until the debt is paid in full. Borrowing money is not a sin, and sometimes, it may be necessary for a business that needs a line of credit. Where we, as consumers, fall short is we tend to pay the minimum payment for months and even let it slide into years. When only the minimum is paid, the interest is, growing by the day.

Say your mortgage payment is $2,000 a month, and while only paying the minimum, it climbs to $2,030 a month. You say to yourself that's not bad, and as time goes by, now you are now staring at $2,100 dollars a month and you have not paid any principal payments. When you are paying the minimum on any bill, it will keep you in debt for years to come.

It goes back to our upbringing, our information, and even application. Who has been teaching you about wealth? Who has been teaching you about planning for retirement? Keep this in mind, because it's important. One day, you will leave your job. You may retire, quit, get fired or die while working, but rest assured the clock is moving fast. Will you be ready for the next chapter of your life?

We must come to the realization that we have been seduced by commercials. YouTube influencers, Instagram and Facebook post of other people's lives and maybe, just maybe, with a little jealousy, we wish it was us taking that selfie in front of a million-dollar home.

As mentioned earlier, building credit does not make you rich; it adds more financial burden to your future. If you don't have the title to your car, it's not yours. Still paying mortgage or line of credit? It belongs to the bank. Please, dear reader, I do understand that the majority of Americans are making good efforts to pay down their debt, but my concern is that we got the memo too late, so we don't like to talk about money or even being debt free. It's the topic that seems to be off limits in many homes in the United States.

Money topics usually come up in emergencies, especially when over seventy percent of families live from paycheck to paycheck. Now, you can put your bills on a credit card; however, in thirty days, you must pay it back. Are you prepared? Do you have six months of savings put away? Do you have life insurance? What will you do if your insurance company does not pay all of your medical expenses? In these scenarios I have just presented, having credit will not get you out of these tight spots.

As consumers, we want it quick and fast. Purchase items, swipe our card and we are gone, no need for receipt, it will be sent out by text message. Then one day while at work, you get a notification that your debit or credit card and your identity has been compromised by someone in Florida who has just brought a 50-inch flat screen with subwoofers in your name. OMG!! Now, the hassle begins. You must get a new card, new number, be put on hold for more than an hour to speak to a representative because there are twenty callers ahead of you.

What is your estimated wait time? I would say about 3 weeks! In 2020, at the height of Covid-19, many businesses stopped taking cash. Why? Well, there were news reports saying that the virus could be transmitted through money. But many biologists and scientists could not find concrete evidence that the virus could be spread through paper money or coins.

So, what we saw in the media made owners panic and they begin to put signs in the window saying 'we don't take cash'. This is a bad business move for retail shop owners because they have now closed off their business to customers who want to pay cash.

That, oddly enough, very few of us, including yours truly, have few clues how it works or if it will benefit our financial future. We just hear it makes a lot of money, but how does it help us? As I mentioned before in this chapter about identity theft, this may be one of the reasons we have not gone to a cashless society yet, because identity theft is on the rise and imagine if all transactions were digital and the servers and Wi-Fi went down even for just a hour, how would this affect the economy?

About a year ago, I needed to go the store and as I went inside, I heard commotion along with angry looks and a lot of profanity. As I glanced over to the cashier station, there was a sign that read 'Cash only, servers are down. Sorry for the inconvenience".

I asked a store clerk, "How long have the servers been down?"

She replied, "About two hours."

As I got my items and left the store, I was driving and noticed to my left, a Wendy's sign in the window that said, 'cash only'. Across the street, McDonald's had the same sign, and then as I stopped at a traffic light, I looked up and saw a Lowe's hardware store. I couldn't believe it! Yes, you can guess, their sign in all caps, CASH ONLY.

Turns out, the servers that supported the businesses all in the same block had crashed. So, while digital currency is easy and fast, long term, it may not make good sense.

For those who are ahead of the game and seem to have no financial concerns, I guarantee you there was a teacher or a strategic plan in place to help them with their goals. As I continue this chapter, I do realize that I may not reach certain demographics, and for the few thousand people who read this, I know there will be questions and concerns, like 'What is this guy talking about? This makes no financial sense!' Like I said before, people don't like to talk about money.

So, let me ask you this question, does credit build wealth? Does having five, six or even seven credit cards give you financial freedom? As you think about your answer, go back to the place where you were taught about financial education. Who told you that you need a credit card for emergencies? What about three months of savings, or using your debit card? These questions should make us all think of how we approach our future, because if you don't act now, you could be facing severe decisions on life, so how will you handle this?

You have good credit but no emergency fund, good credit but you owe thousands on four credit cards, behind on mortgage, medical bills and your mind is racing with thoughts of doubt and fear and possibly desperation because you realize that your choices have caught up with you. Oh, it took a while, but it's here; reality is knocking at your door and you are not ready. This is chilling. It makes me think of my grandmother. She retired at the age of sixty-two, and when she did, I had no idea she didn't have a pension, very little savings, just social security. She did odd jobs, domestic work in Madison Park for very wealthy people, and even got a paper route at sixty-two so she could raise me, but we never talked about retirement or how money works.

We had the occasional talks about putting money away and savings, but the most valuable advice she gave me was don't get a credit card.

This advice was golden!

I always wondered why when I went into my local bank, the teller would always want to me to sign up for a credit card. "Mr. Burney, Mr. Burney, sir, we noticed you don't have a credit and we can provide you a very low interest rate and get you a platinum card right away. Would you like to sign up today?"

My reply? "No, thank you."

Now, this conversation continued for many transactions, until one teller told me my approach to money was unconventional, but she also mentioned that it was smart.

I then realized they were only doing what they were taught, be it by job description or on-site classes, most tellers in the banks are not taught how to help people become debt free.

Not long after this, they left me alone. They tried the same tactic on Terri but to no avail. We held our ground.

So, you have to build wealth from the ground up. Here we go. First, start where you are and map out a plan. Start by gathering every single bill you have and make up your mind that these bills cannot live in your house anymore. You must put yourself on a budget and have someone hold you accountable about your financial choices.

Excuse me for going off script for a moment, but this will make sense (I hope).

A coworker of mine came up to me and said, "Uncle George, can you help me with money?"

I said, "Maybe, how can I help you?" Note, this is totally unorthodox, but somehow it worked.

For about eight months, every payday, she came by my work area and gave me $200. And when she quit, there was a few thousand dollars. I gave it back to her. Please, please, do not try this method at home, work or anywhere. I feel better now. I then asked her, "What are you going to do with the money?"

She said, "I don't know, Uncle."

I suggested that she buy mutual and index funds and explained that over time, this will build wealth for her and her family. When fears take over you can find yourself asking people who have no financial education for help while this advice was unorthodox it did help this young lady change her mindset about how wealth works

Building wealth takes time; having a high credit score does nothing to help you financially. Let me just park here for a minute. The key reason why banks are so successful? Marketing, advertising using A list celebrities who are influential, all so you can get points? Or two percent cash back on your purchases at the store.

Financial guru Dave Ramsey, who has helped thousands of people get out of debt, went on a rant in 2019 with "Think, America". It is on YouTube and has over 422,000 views. While his approach was loud and sometimes comical in his presentation, it was on point as he pleaded with his audience to make better choices in their financial choices. He told his viewers, "Do you know how you get back $1,000 from Chase bank? You spend $100,000 dollars! Where in the world did you do your math?" Also, in this classic rant, he said, "Do you know how you get rid of Sallie Mae? You either pay her off in full or you die!"

In 2015, Terri and I met Dave Ramsey in person. We were part of the VIP access group who were invited for dinner and a Q& A session. It was a turnaround for our financial education as I was able to ask questions from a man who was and still is debt free. He said, "Sir, you ask questions like a journalist or tv reporter."

While I appreciated the comment, on that night, I was trying to learn everything I could about investing, budgeting and retirement. It was an epic moment in time for me.

It is crucial that you make steps toward your goals before it's too late. In my last book, I mentioned how I let my manuscript about my grandmother sit on a shelf for over a decade before I took action you cannot continue to spend with no budget and continue to put off financial planning until you are sixty-five. Time is of the essence.

Credit scores are basically like a report card, but this report card is like no other. It's not just your parents who see your credit grade, the whole world is all in your business. Their job (banks) is to help you build your credit, not to plan your retirement, because as your credit score rises, the doors open. Like the platinum door, the gold door, the black card door, and once those doors are open, your credit score rises and so does your debt, and the more debt you create, the more time you shave off your future, the more stress you create for your family, and you even put your health as risk because what debt does is give you a whole new set of problems.

What would it be like to have no car payments?

No mortgage payments? Keep this in mind, until

your house or car is paid in full, it's not yours. It

belongs to the bank.

Reading this book is a pivotal moment in your

life. What are you going to do? Get mad, make

excuses? Blame it on your educational

background?

The time for action is now. In my last book, I

mentioned how Terri and I were down to $93. It

was crushing to us; however, we did not fall to

the practice of getting a credit card. Why? Well,

we knew one day, it would be over. We also

realized that what was stolen from us was not

going to be given back. The nature of a thief is to take, run and hide. The lawyer who took $420,000 from us was not going to give this money back, so as time went on, we started getting information on how to get our financial years back, rolling up our sleeves, cutting back on what we did not need, making sacrifices for our 401k planning, being intentional about our giving and helping those in need, and putting away an emergency fund, just in case.

We continue to build wealth and not credit. Remember, the borrower is slave to the lender. You cannot borrow your way to wealth. You can borrow money but you can't borrow time.

Chapter 3

Who Taught You About Financial Literacy?

I still find it hard to believe why financial education is not taught in the public school system. So, if this is the case, who is teaching you about your financial future? In many cases, it's our parents or grandparents who did not have the right tools to pass down to the next generation. What this means is by the time we get our first job, we really don't have a generational plan because we just spend, spend, work and repeat. My grandmother taught me a masterclass about saving and responsibility when I got my first job at Safeway and I got my first check. About a month earlier, I had passed my driver's test and was ready to hit the mall.

As I headed out the door, she said, "George, please come here for a few moments. I have something for you."

I was like, *what does she want now.* Now, of course, I said this to myself because when I was coming along, you didn't show disrespect to you parents or grandparents.

As I walked in the dining room, she told me to sit down. My eyes directly went to a long piece of notebook paper. As I looked closely, the words on the paper were actually a list that read, 'rent, phone, lights and car'. My lips started to quiver and I said, "Momma? What is this?"

She said, "This is responsibility."

I said, "Momma, my responsibility?"

So there went my first check. As I headed out the door to go to the mall, I was drained, and she told me if I had a problem with this to let her know. So, that's what I did for five years. I helped pay utilities, phone, and brought food into the home. Remember the karate kid movie? Wax on, wax off. Well, five years later, I turned twenty-one and was so excited, but I was in shock when my grandmother gave me a really nice watch which I still have today. I was overcome with emotion when she gave me a check. Yes, you already know where I am going. It was the money I had put into the home, paying bills all those years. Wax on, wax off—what a teaching moment that was.

With all the technology and online classes and YouTube universities we have been flooded with, TMI—too much information—where do we go for sound advice and reliable education? As I get older, I realize how important staying in your lane is. Somehow, everyone has a hot stock tip or a great multilevel marketing plan, but the majority of these dreams do not get fulfilled, or even take off, because the information is inadequate, doesn't add up, and when we realize that this is the wrong way, we become frustrated. Believe it or not you can apply the wrong principles to your dream. What is vital in that moment is to realize that you must recover, and do it quickly. Surround yourself with talented people, with character, integrity, not those who just want to flaunt and flex.

Yes, homes and cars in today's society are essentials, just like water and other essentials that you and I need. However, there must be a purpose with your wealth.

The Q and A Session

I recently talked to my goddaughter and asked her what financial freedom meant to her When I received her answers, it was heartfelt and on point.

Our goddaughter, Kimberly, is in graduate school and just recently purchased a home with her brother.

"Financial independence, to me, means having the ability or privilege to live comfortably, whatever that means to you. I don't mean buying a private jet or a big mansion because you can but, I mean the freedom to be sound and secure with day-to-day real LIFE. Maybe it's buying coffee every morning and not having to think about the cost, or it could be having a savings account with enough money in there to last 3 to 6 months in the event of an emergency or in a medical emergency. It could also mean to have the ability to purchase real estate within in your means and I don't mean buying an island. I guess what I am trying to say is financial independence, means having peace of mind that if something were to happen, you would be okay."

She also continued her answer by saying who taught her about money. "My parents, Mom and Dad, taught me about budgeting, credit, what

NOT to do, how to write a check, how to apply for a credit card and how to read a bank statement. They taught me pretty early in life because of their own financial struggles and mistakes. I've always thought financial education should be built into the school system, starting in elementary school all the way to college. I am in my thirties and I am discovering things about money that I had no idea about and would have loved to have known years ago. I think some of that had to do with my parents' financial journey and the disadvantages middle class families and families of color face in this country.

Kimberly said, "Financial freedom is having the means to not only purchase necessities, but also additional comforts. I don't ever recall receiving advice on financial literacy. I do believe that these lessons would have been invaluable in preparing me for college, home ownership and adulthood overall."

Once again, I love this answer; it shows how important education is.

What families need is education about money from experts in their fields. Where the disconnect comes from is that people who are wealthy have the right people teaching them and their families. The right people in your life are key in every area of your life. Whom you choose as your friends, the people you work with, they all matter.

In the workplace, the employee is hired according to their resume, but do you have the "right person" because their resume is exceptional? Consider these questions. in your circle of friends and family, how many of them are debt free? How do your friends spend their time? Do you talk about your goals? Or do you talk about others? Usually, wealthy people talk about ideas, while poor people talk about each other. Now, depending on how you perceive these last few sentences, you're probably thinking POOR!! What is George trying to say?

He writes a book and now he is a financial guru?

No, this is not what I am saying. I am trying to get you to do some critical thinking by looking at these words, and maybe an epiphany will take place.

Usually, when the truth is presented to us, we reject it. Why? But we are comfortable in our pain, used to being average, not curious anymore about what's on the other side of mediocrity, and so that's where most people stay—the comfort zone, the La-Z Boy chair.

Meanwhile, the clock is ticking; not only are you getting older, but so is your dream. It's getting gray hair, its vision is growing dim and then, eventually, we put our dreams on hold, then we put them to sleep.

Let's move slightly into social media topics, where there are some influencers who do give sound advice. For the last three years, the financial trending topic for millennials has been minimalist. While not taking a vow of poverty, they are cutting back on buying things in excess. Over-the-top purchases are not on their radar but, rather, putting away for the future of their children. Perhaps this is a more meaningful life for younger people, who now, in the 21st century, have record salaries in the tech world and seem to be lured into paying $3,500 a month for an apartment. Let's do the math here. At $3,500 a month, for one year, that will be $42,000. If, by chance, they stay in their apartment for three years, it will cost them $120,000. Remember, when you lease or rent, that apartment is not yours; you are actually helping the owners of the apartment pay off the loan they took out to build those one hundred units.

Condominiums or apartments? I am not sure how they got this one past us, but for some reason, it's been working. For decades now, condominiums are selling as homes, prices ranging from the low 300,000 dollar range all the way up to the 800,000 dollar range. So, you have a $300,000 condominium about 900 square ft, one bedroom, one bathroom and a kitchen that's so small, you have to go into the living room to turn around! What you have, my friend, is an apartment.

In an online article in 2019, Jousha Fields and Mill-burn Ryan Nicodemus, who are minimalists, made the world sit up and take notice with their article entitled "11 signs you might be poor" (1) You live from paycheck to paycheck. (2) You have credit card debt. (3) You also have student loan debt. (4) You have monthly car payment. (5)

Your income dictates your lifestyle. (6) You are not saving for the future. (7) You are not healthy. (8) Your relationships are suffering. (9) You argue over money. (10) You are not growing. (11) You don't contribute as much as you should.

As I read this periodical, what stood out to me were numbers (6) and (7). This is powerful because, if you are not saving for the future, it means you have no goals, no vision. Is it because of fear that you are not putting away for your future? Or maybe you were not given the tools you needed for success.

Number 7, you are not healthy. You have heard the quote 'your health is your wealth'. That statement right there should all make us realize how important life is. While the majority of this book is on financial education, please note, if your health is failing, then your money cannot save you This is why, as Americans, we should look at our health as an investment and not a burden. And in the end, not having your health will cost you more money in the long run.

I did not see this in the article, but I want to add number 12. You don't have a plan. As I am writing this second book, I can look up from my desk and see index cards and post-it notes, and also at least twenty books on self-help, my Bible,

five other books on financial education and five

others on fitness and nutrition. Usually, I am up

at 3am, with my notes in front of me and my to-

do list as I plan my day and the months ahead.

Why? One word, Terri. If I don't plan, then she

will not be taken care of.

As a younger man, I did not know how

important my future would be, but I believe

now, I have clear vision of how important

financial literacy is.

Let me go back to how important financial

education is. The average investor goes into the

stock market blindly, not knowing if single

stocks are a good choice, or maybe he or she is

trying to move into mutual funds or index funds.

What may seem like a good idea at the time,

could possibly put you and your family at risk.

There are some Americans who might take a

chance on YouTube or maybe even Facebook,

and what comes between those videos are ads

(author break, I don't like ads) it's known as click

bait, where you will see someone with about

$10,000 in cash and according to them, you can

make this quickly with no education, no money

down, no experience, and with a resounding

voice you will hear this, "We do all the work for

you." And then your mind starts to wonder, *is this possible?*

The majority of the ads you and I see from companies have to do with you, the customer. Their ads are designed to make you believe that your life will be better with this product.

Earlier in this book, you read that money is not being taught in the public schools. This is alarming because when the students become of age and graduate, they are really not ready for life. A degree, they have, but it's investment tools that they need. Also, we have to remind ourselves that education has totally changed; the bachelor and master's degrees don't hold the leverage they use to. While these academic measures are very important and we all want skilled workers, what we find is that the degrees that are held by thousands of graduates are now becoming obsolete, and to add more pressure to the graduates, their student loans are making their future look dim. I am not really big on conspiracy theory; however, I do believe that there's vital information being held back from the middle class and poor. Is this on purpose? Maybe. Is there some agenda to keep the majority of U.S. citizens poor? Maybe. Or could it be our educators? The one student grade 1 through 12 never got the money memo. Why?

Because it was never taught. How can you be held accountable or take responsibility for something that you were never taught? You don't even realize that you are heading blindly into the world without direction or a map. This is serious, because if you are not on point about generational wealth, your children and grandchildren and possibly your great grandchildren will fall into the same mindset and when asked about money, they will say, "I learned about money from my mom and dad." It would be a smart move to hire a financial planner to teach your children the value of money and how to use it wisely.

Reflection

_____

_____

_____

_____

_____

_____

_____

_____

_____

_____

_____

_____

_____

_____

_____

_____

_____

_____

_____

_____

_____

Chapter 4

Where Does Your Money Go?

"Show me your receipts and I will show you where your money goes."

George Burney

This is a question most Americans ask every two weeks, because working eighty hours every two weeks, getting paid on Friday, and shaking your head on Monday while your brain is trying to figure out where your paycheck went can be frustrating.

This is where budgeting comes into play. You have to tell your money where to go, find a good budgeting app and follow the plan. Most apps are easy to use. You put in the amount you are paid every two weeks minus your expenses, and this will give insight on how to watch your spending habits. As a young child, I never could figure out why seniors always wanted receipts. Back in the day, when you went to the grocery store, you always heard the loud sound of the cash registers as the cashiers quickly looked at all the food items, making sure that there were no mistakes. And at the end of transaction, I would always see a long piece of register tape come up and my grandmother quickly looked to see if she had been overcharged. When we got home, she had me put away the food while she went into the dining room with the receipt and a pen and a pair of reading glasses, to see if she somehow got overcharged. This chapter might be helpful and, hopefully, encouraging to you on how money works.

Consider this: in the next two weeks, starting on the Friday you get paid, start keeping your receipts for the next two weeks. Be it cash, debit or credit cards, cash app or seller, keep your phone alert on and when you spend money, make sure you get a text message. Here is something that should get your attention, STARBUCKS.

According to cliffandpebble.com the average consumer will have spent over $7,000 a year on Starbucks, and if you multiply that by five years, that will be $35,000. Receipts add up. Your trip to the store? Well, before you go, make a shopping list. This is what seniors used to do which, at the time, seemed old-school and outdated. Cable TV, Hulu, live streaming Netflix, can you hear the cash register ringing now? Yes, this is where your money is going. Children? Aging parents, vacations, trips to the casino? Let me park here for a moment. The casino, for some, can be an allure, all of the amenities and restaurants at reasonable prices, free drinks, penny slots, all the bells and whistles. And before you know it, you could find yourself there on a Friday night, and that would be a payday Friday night, walking into the casino with a feeling, and once you pull that lever, it's like electricity going through your body. Two hours later, you're still there and your reasonable sense is nowhere to be found. Remember, you have a mortgage and two kids who will soon be in college, but you're trying to find a reasonable excuse to why you should stay there.

Dear reader, in no way am I condemning you or judging your decision. I would like you to reconsider your choices of trying to make fast money.

Now, back to the receipts. When the next payday comes around, take all your receipts and put them on the table, get your calculator out and start adding the numbers. Divide them into two categories. (1) necessities (2) things you wanted. or the next two weeks, cut back on what you wanted. I am quite sure by doing this, you will have more money left over.

The online magazine Investopedia gave a very good synopsis of where most Americans spend their money. Food at home $4,464, food away from home $3459, apparel and miscellaneous services $3975, car purchase $3,975, gasoline $2,100, personal care products $768 and entertainment $3,226.

These stats seem a little different. It could mean the quarterly, but it's a clear indication of where your money is going.

There are consumers who will spend without thinking about the consequences of their "now" choices. But when tomorrow comes, that's when the ringtone in their heart reminds them, *I should have waited. I should have listened.* Playing catch-up in life is exhausting and expensive; it will cost you a lot more down the road. This is why, in sports, when you see NFL teams or nab teams that are behind in the game, their hopes are in the second half because they get a chance to catch up, a chance to redeem themselves with a renewed hope. If, by chance, you are reading this book and over the age of forty-five, you are in the second half of life. There is hope, but your actions must be with intent and seeking out the right information. What usually brings back a sports team from losing in the first half is momentum, and they play with intensity as the clock starts ticking away. First, you must write down a budget and a spreadsheet and begin to pencil in where your dollars are going. Also, it would wise and crucial to get a financial planner to help you to catch up. There are good financial planners who are the best in their field and can guide you and assist you in catching up in your retirement, and also plan for your other goals that you may want to share with your family.

Fidelity Investments T.D. Ameritrade not only help with retirement, but can service your needs when it comes to personal finances.

A few years ago, I talked to my financial planner and she began to ask me a series of questions. As I began to give her the answers, my brain was going, *why do you need to know all of this?* I didn't realize that, on her end, she was creating a financial chart for me and a stat sheet that would help me get closer to my goals. Investments, at the beginning, are slow and mundane; like a turtle with four broken legs, it's barely moving!! But when it (401k Roth) begins to peak, you find yourself going, *oh, this is what I've been waiting for!* When it comes to investments, there will be some things you will have to sacrifice, because in order to achieve this goal, you must give up some spending habits temporarily. Perhaps your most important investment is your health. If you don't invest in yourself, you will not be able to take care of your family. In a recent CNBC report, it was noted that most Americans by the year 2023 will spend at less $14,000 a year on medical bills. Their data from centers for Medicare and Medicaid is eye opening because the year 2023 will be here shortly. So, keep this in mind. In order to achieve your goals, you must invest in your health; prevention is key. We have all heard this before, but it still holds true today that eating right, exercise, getting the right amount of sleep and managing stress will possibly extend your life. When we go to the store and make our choices, we are actually making an investment, we just don't realize it. When our doctors give us a plan and it's mapped out with important information on how to obtain better health, the doctor is actually investing in us; we just have to choose our destiny. So, where does our money go? Well, according to this CNBC report, it will go to medical bills.

Consider this. Investing in your health now pays huge dividends more than any material things will. Keep in mind, it will cost you to pay for better health, but it's the mindset we must look at. Food, vitamins, gym membership, or exercise equipment at home, be it Peloton, Nordic track, resistance bands, or detox cleanses, they are all here to help us. A few chapters ago, I focused on credit cards, how they affect spending habits of consumers. What it does physiologically, is disconnects the buyer (at certain times) from making sound choices about their future.

Think about it, you walk into a retail store in the mall or you buy items online, you point, you click and you buy, but do you think? Is this a necessity? Is this in my budget? Will this purchase affect my future? The old saying of 'your health is your wealth' is so very powerful. Your wellbeing is vital to carrying out your dreams, and a healthy mindset will allow you to help others to achieve their dreams as well.

These next few lines will help us all think about how we spread our paychecks. Please keep in mind that this book is to change our mindset, not to criticize, but rather to help us be aware of our future

Here we go. In a recent online article, the ascent, which is an association with the "Motley Fool", gave an eye-opening account of how consumers overspend.

Let's look at it more closely. Seventy-six percent of consumers pay excessive fees, mostly late fees. Seventy-three percent on impulse buying. Sixty-eight percent, using unnecessary energy in their homes. Sixty-six percent waste money on luxury items. Do you see now where your money is going? Wait, there's more. Fifty-five percent waste money on digital services. Forty-eight percent overpay for beverages, fifty-two percent throw out food or expired food unnecessarily, forty-four percent of consumers' money goes to fast food, and lastly, forty-seven percent of consumers' money goes to upgrades on functional items that really could last a few more years. The bottom line is you must tell your money where to go, because without a plan, you will just spend and spend without thinking about your tomorrow.

Reflection

_____

_____

_____

_____

_____

_____

_____

_____

_____

_____

_____

_____

_____

_____

_____

_____

_____

_____

_____

_____

_____

_____

Chapter 5

Marketing, Social Media And Spending Habits

When Covid-19 came along, the world came to a pause. I remember as I went to work in the morning, the streets were quiet. Only the streetlights above gave evidence of the quiet road beneath, no headlights of cars, no traffic jams, the commute to work was seamless. This was not a dream or a PSA announcement.

COVID is REAL.

This pandemic caught everyone off guard. The malls were shut down, and sporting events held their games in stadiums that had little to no fans.

What this did was reveal who had a plan and who didn't have a plan. What I find amazing and jaw dropping is that Amazon's profits soared over two-hundred percent last year.

People were losing their jobs, companies were shutting down, unemployment and furloughs were being offered to millions around the United States, but the focus somehow was on retail spending.

It is difficult to understand the spending habits of others, maybe it's scientific or impulse. But believe it or not, marketing and social media play a huge roll in perception. And social media really has allowed us to live a life online that, in reality, is not truthful. Take note. All Instagram accounts and Twitter accounts will give you access to someone's world for about sixty seconds, and it's within that timeframe where they (content creators) must capture your attention. The goal is to get you to believe that your life will be better with their products or somehow your life is not completely satisfactory unless you click that link. And when you click the link, that is where you get trapped. I really never have been a fan of commercials or ads on YouTube. I always hit the "skip ads" and watch the video. It's amazing how advertisers can now make a ten second ad to reel the curious retailers in.

I would encourage you to STOP AND THINK before you buy, because if you don't, your future could be derailed because you did not take a few moments to think things out.

In your money goals, you must be specific and you must have a plan of how to reach those goals when your plan starts to become a burden. What are your goals for the future? How much money do you need to live off? Will you have enough put away for a rainy day? Yes, it will rain and your storm will blow, but will you be covered? Here's a question that will get you to think and even say "really?".

How much money did Doritos pay for a thirty second ad in the 2021 super bowl? (a) 600,000) (b) one-point-five million or (c) six million. Yeah, six million dollars was the price tag, and where do companies get their money? That would be you, the customer, and keep in mind that advertisers have pivoted to other social media platforms, and in order to get you and me involved, the thirty second commercial spot turns into a miniseries as they run the thirty second ad on national TV. Then they will say, "Tune in to YouTube to see the rest of the story."

This marketing is researched just by observation of consumers' choices. Do you remember when ranch dressing was actually for salad? And how did McDonald's get the name Mickey D's?

The art of the marketing is simple now; you're understanding how consumers will spend money. What are they mostly likely to buy? Years ago, Microsoft came out with a product that was to compete with Apple's iPod; it was called Zune. Multi-millions were spent on research and marketing for this product that was going to possibly be an iPod killer. The results were not good, and eventually, the Zune was pulled from the market. You can advertise, edit and re-edit, but if the people don't respond with sales, it's going to make or break a company. One of the reasons Apple has such success is their company is not just about their marketing, it has a lot to do with their products. Steve Jobs literally changed the world we live in and his vision was to make life better, but keep in mind that Jobs did not do this by himself. He surrounded himself with others who were smarter than he was. And this is how you will succeed in financial planning—if you surround yourself with the people who are smarter than you, not only smarter, but those who have integrity and are willing to help you with your financial goals. And because of Jobs, consumers would actually wait outside for days in the cold or heat to get a phone. People will actually get up early for Black Friday and stand in line for hours. The key word here is sacrifice and the question is why? Our spending habits say a lot about us. How we plan for the future tells us where our priorities are. What is working against the American workers is leverage; it always seems to elude those who are trying to make a better life. Let me remember the quote again from the mathematician, 'To live effectively is to live a life with adequate information'. That quote right there should reset your thinking when it comes to life. This is where educational programs in our schools and lives play a key role in setting up our children for successful living. What is missing is getting the tools to enhance listening. When a student starts from first grade to twelfth grade without financial education, they are already more than a decade behind on their future. Our spending habits are triggered by our behavior, and in order to change our behavior, we must first change our mindset. That is why education is key in the lives of our young people. The less you know, the farther behind you will begin life. So since we were not taught about financial education from the first grade to the twelfth grade, we are twelve years behind, and if our parents were not taught about money, it puts us generations behind. Our spending habits are not inherited, but taught to us by good meaning people with inadequate information, and if not caught early, the next three to five generations will be left without wealth building tools. At the time of writing this chapter, the holidays are vastly approaching and soon Christmas will be on upon us. The Covid numbers are dropping, the malls are starting once again to swelling up with shoppers who are eager to spend their money.

So, let's fast forward to 2022, January, to be exact. Your first credit card bill has arrived and there it is, an outline and description of what you spent for Christmas.

Now, what happens? Will you be paying this bill off or will you be like most consumers and only pay the minimum every month? During the holidays, marketers pour millions into advertising, counting on you to swipe yourself into debt, because it's such a part of our culture that most people believe gifts can only be purchased at the mall or online.

What about spending time with your grandchildren or maybe volunteering at a senior home? How about teaching your nieces and nephews about financial literacy?

Use your talent and education to teach others about retirement accounts. Does this sound like a gift? Probably not, because the average person does not incline their thoughts toward financial education, and these last few sentences you are reading have no traction to the thought process. If not caught in its early stages, your spending habits will rob you of your future.

There are quick ways to make money, but getting wealth not earned can leave you without a future. I hope that this book would get you to rethink your position about wealth and what it means to you. It's not about just leaving your family with millions of dollars, but rather making sure their future is secured.

Three, years ago Terri and I purchased our first home, and as we were looking at homes, our real estate agent Carol guided us. As we were counting up the costs, I believed that we had enough to pay for a nice home. Carol took us to this home and as we walked through the door, it was beautiful, high ceilings, state of the art kitchen washer and dryer upstairs and downstairs, a bathtub inside the shower. I was in shock but ready to buy.

Now, this is where wisdom comes in. My real estate agent, the best in her field, asked me one question, "George, do you really need a $900,000 home?" She went on to say, "Let's see if we can look at other choices." She saved us over $400,000 and years of heartache. My ignorance about financial literacy had already cost me $420,000 once, and if you read my first book, you will know we went into a real estate deal blindly. But this time was different; we actually had the right person in our lives who guided us in the right direction.

Having the right people in your life, is vital. The character of your real estate agent is a must. The teacher who shapes the young minds of our children is essential. The doctors, lawyers, and politicians, along with athletes, must take responsibility for the people they have influence over. Your circle of friends and how they treat you and your family matters. Who is your circle of friends? How do they affect your life, and do they play an important role in your life when it comes to your finances? It is amazing that retailers and credit card companies know how to separate you from your future. Let's think this out for a minute. When you sign up for a credit card, your information is now on a database that is shared and reshared again. So now, your information is stored in the cloud, and then before you know it, you are receiving more mail in your inbox. Remember that retailers and banks now know about your spending habits, and before you know it, you have purchased thousands of dollars in one click. But wait a minute, your conscience reminds you that your mortgage bill will be in your mailbox in a few days. So, this all goes back to the question, where did we go wrong? How did we get here? And is there a way for anyone to live without debt? These questions can be debated and they might even may good subject for a podcast, but what is at stake here is making up for lost time.

This can be frustrating, because time cannot be returned once it's gone. There is no going back. Take note. Has it ever occurred to you that most staff meetings always have their attention on old business? The meeting can go on for hours without a resolution, and after a motion is made to table old business, the meeting is over but the problem remains.

This is why construction projects are delayed and some retailers have to close their doors. It's because they have spent too much time on old business. And when time is spent on old business, there is no problem solved, the future is quickly evaporating

There is another reason why we have gotten off track. It's hard for us to address that past wounds don't heal until they get addressed. But be it in a corporation or an employee in the workplace, leadership often avoids the steps to address matters and correct them. They get buried in red tape and fear because, often times, people are afraid to speak up. Let me go off track for just a moment. It's not just consumers who are behind in paying bills; the United States of America has a national debt in the trillions of dollars. America cannot pay her bills. And as of December 2023, Americans are now 3 trillion dollars in credit card debt. Our country gives to the poor, we help other nations in times of trouble, when earthquakes and disaster break out, we respond. But for some reason, we cannot seem to solve the homeless crisis. Why is it that taxes continue to be increased and there are times at the voting polls, we will vote for a tax hike, hoping that it will help our schools and infrastructure? We pay property taxes on our homes, and the money is divided into certain categories that should make our neighborhoods better, but it seems as if we never have a surplus. Our infrastructure here in the United States is behind other countries. Is it possible that

America doesn't have a plan for the future, or is

the plan we have in the wrong hands?

Chapter 6

Will Your Job Be Around In Five Years?

"If you don't find a way to make money in your sleep, you will work until you die." Warren Buffet

A few years back, there was a movement in the United States that involved the majority of retail workers and people who also worked in hotels and fast food chains. The $15 an hour Now slogan gained traction as the whole nation was listening to the concerns of workers, who were only making around $13 dollars an hour. Other states' minimum wages started out around $8 an hour. Most of these hard-working people could not make ends meet as some Americans took on two jobs so they could take care of their families. When you add the numbers up, a full-time job making $15 an hour is still right at the poverty level. This proposal was finally passed in most of the United States, and the majority of franchise owners were not happy about it because now, their margins would begin to sink. This time was a short-lived victory, because now in 2022, automation has sprung up and fast food franchises like McDonald's has partnered with IBM to create artificial intelligence in their drive-thru, which would eliminate the need for at least three people.

The working class could be on their way to extinction. Believe it or not, there are robots that can actually clean hotel rooms. Some giant retailers have robots go down the aisle after the store closes and the robot actually does the inventory and orders products for the whole store. All of this took years of planning; it didn't just pop up overnight. And if you think about it, the workforce will not be entirely eliminated, but it will definitely shrink the work force in the coming years. What is catching most of us off guard is not being prepared for change. We hear conversations about the future, but somehow we think that it will not affect us or our family. Before you know it, the future is here but we have not planned for it. Wealthy people are not too rattled about change or even concerned when the stock market starts to sink. Why? Because their planning and being around the right people who are educated in the area of investing has allowed them to see how money works, and when there is a major change in the economy, wealthy people do not get overly concerned.

In Dr. Myles Munroe's book "The Principles And Benefits Of Change," he writes on how we all can benefit from change in our lives. He says, 'If you don't learn to accept change, you will inevitably react to it when it occurs. You won't be able to respond effectively. A clear understanding that life will change is the key to preparing and planning for times of transition. It is this response of preparation that will give you control over change.'

That quote by Dr Munroe actually made me less fearful of change, knowing that all change is not bad if you prepare for your tomorrow. Changes on your job may still be around in five years; however, the job description will look different and you will have fewer coworkers. What employees must keep in mind is that we are replaceable. It doesn't matter how many times you have been employee of the month or your years of service. It is rare to see or hear of a high-ranking CEO who has a plan to keep employees around. While we are not planning for the future, the CEO is mapping out a twenty-year plan for the company, and the bottom line is cost. To be fair, there are some companies that do value the work of their employees and try to map out a plan that includes them, but there are other employers who will replace workers with automation and call this improvement. This is why you must have a plan in place for your tomorrow. While you are reading this book, your employer is in a boardroom with the CEO and outside contractors as they offer bids at a lower rate. They are making moves, and they do not include you. The best way to adapt to change is to get on board, surround yourself with people who are more intelligent than you and who are the brilliant in their field. Stay away from the conspiracy critic and the 'woe is me' person. You cannot spend time rehashing the same old things from five years ago. While some points may be valid and true, the question is what are you going to do about it? Do you have a plan or a solution? Or just an opinion?

The majority of jobs that we see today are not going away, but they are evolving. To the factory work or to the cashier whose job is now being automated, it definitely looks like elimination. As a young boy, I remember our neighbor who killed himself because his position at work was being eliminated and fifty of his coworkers were being let go. He was depressed, and without retirement and with mounting bills, he saw no way out. Perception is key to how you look at your struggles. In the 1960s, my grandmother worked at Boeing and she was excited because she had just graduated, receiving her electronic assembly degree. But in 1968, there were massive layoffs at Boeing and she and about a hundred of her colleagues were laid off. This did not detour her, however, because I was her "why." I was seven years old at the time. I was her reason why she recovered so quickly.

So, when you get out of bed in the morning, you must ask yourself, "What is my why? Who am I doing this for? How many people are depending on me today?" Many people count on you not to give up. Don't look at it like how can I do this, have the mindset I get to do this!! And with this mindset, you will think more clearly about your goals. Education is key to a bright future, and having the right teachers in your life can set you up for accomplishments. The majority of jobs we work are not designed to shape us into leaders.

We are given a job description and we learn to follow the rules. And when we are stuck in a certain mindset, we do not often question the rules that are set before us, not realizing that the workplace rules often don't benefit our growth. Once again, let me clarify this passage. I'm not saying that you should violate company policy, because without guidelines in the work place, there is no order. My concern is does your job allow you to grow? Or does it give you a feeling of being trapped? Traps are designed to keep you in place; being debt-free releases you from the uncertainty of how you will live.

Chapter 7

Debt Kills Dreams

"Debt puts you in a choke hold and will not let

your future breathe."

George Burney

My ignorance on financial matters may not

allow me to write with the intelligence that I

should. I am not a financial planner. But I do

have a message that you should listen to. Would

you please take note—debt kills dreams like

sugar kills the immune system. When debt

becomes part of our lives, we seldom realize that

it actually is taking away our future. It has

become part of the family, but we don't talk

about it, just like we don't talk about our crazy relatives, because we are embarrassed by them, so we just don't tell them and avoid them at all costs. By avoiding debt and not talking about a plan to eliminate it, we are setting ourselves up for disaster.

Everyone we know has a dream for a better life and goals they are trying to reach, but without the proper advisor, it's like throwing darts and hoping you hit the target.

While we are arguing amongst ourselves and pointing fingers at politicians, our dreams are fading, which should make us all rethink our positions on who is right or wrong.

What debt does to your future is alarming. It affects every area of your life and it crushes your aspirations. I am an avid sports fan, football, baseball, basketball and tennis. I love to see athletes at the top of their field competing for a championship.

It is also saddened to see the aging athlete who does not know his or her time has passed. It comes down to their advisors and who is on their team. Knowing when to walk away, is a crucial component, because if you overstay your welcome, life will escort you on to your next chapter whether you are ready are not. Several years ago, ESPN filmed a documentary called

BROKE. It was brilliant storytelling as many NFL and NBA players told their story of how they went from millions of dollars to filing bankruptcy. What stood out to me about each athlete was they all said, 'I did not follow the advice of my team.' These athletes were going into restaurant business, carwash business, real estate deals. They had the money, but the key component was missing, wisdom. After less than three years of retirement, more than seventy-five percent of professional athletes go broke and have nothing left for their futures.

The most exciting event for an athlete is their first contract signing where, with the stroke of a pen, they are instant millionaires. What a moment that is! And as the cameras are rolling and the contracts are being signed, behind these young, talented athletes, are family members, and in the same room, are sponsors and even tax attorneys, all with a different mindset.

In the BROKE documentary, the athletes were honest as they said they would carry $10,000 to $30,000 around in cash; another $20,000, they kept around the house. After buying their parents a home and buying cars and jewelry and investments, they didn't understand their balance, like their careers were just about to make an exit, but the road they were heading to was a dead end. Money, for many Americans, is a tough subject to discuss. It is a topic only brought up when it's too late. Perception sometimes keeps many people from keeping an open mind about how economy works in the American home. What we hear a lot of is good debt vs. bad debt, but isn't all debt bad? As I wrote earlier, I do understand that at certain times, you will have to borrow money, but once you go into that area, it can very well cost you your future. In the old testament scriptures, in reads, "The borrower is slave to the lender." Also in the scriptures, it reminds us that the rich rule over the poor. Becoming a slave to debt, can lead to generational poverty. Poverty is not just in dollars and cents, but a poverty mindset can also be handed down from generation to generation. In order for your dreams to be manifested, there must be a plan put into place. It is sad when a family member passes away, but what brings more stress is when a relative has no will. It's like having no instructions for your future. This why planning is so very important. Wealthy people have plans; poor people have fights. If no will is in place, it means that the hospital and the state will make the decisions about your loved ones, and without a plan in place, you will find that families will be forced to make choices without clear instructions. Debt also affects your health. The mental stress of trying to get ahead and paying off a thirty-year mortgage, as well as paying for your children's college education, and the bills just keep mounting. For years, the number one killer in America has been heart disease. In that top ten list, you will find depression and hypertension. However, stress seems to be absent from most of these top ten lists. This is another topic that is often overlooked. Stress is repackaged as being in a funk or just feeling tired or maybe not getting enough sleep.

All of these things are important when it comes to our health, but some stress can be less impactful if there's a plan in place. There is no freedom in debt. It puts your dreams into a choke hold and it will not let your future breath. As of now, at 10:03pm, November 5th, 2021, I am sitting in my office with many questions running through my mind. Will I have enough to retire? Will my job be outsourced? Do I have enough money in my emergency fund? If you are honest with yourself, you probably have had those questions and hundreds more. It's like the energy meter on the side of your house that just keeps spinning without destination, and what is frustrating is that you don't have the answers that you need. And this is what is missing. Advice, advice that leads you and your family to a better future. Wisdom that will make you rethink how you make your decisions. Let's call them wisdom choices. Wisdom is more valuable than wealth; it can save the future of your family, and if applied correctly, it very well may set up your children, grandchildren, and great-grandchildren for a better life. So, where did we go wrong? How did our families, with all this knowledge in the 21st century, wind up struggling to make ends meet? (sidebar, ends don't meet)

You cannot be so comfortable with debt to the point you let it live with you like an uninvited guest; you must be intentionally focused on how to get rid of debt for good. Earlier in this book, I presented to you how schools do not teach financial education. This is concerning because, if this the case, by the time your children are twelve years behind and since their parents were not taught about money, this puts them generations behind. This is why most families seem to always be playing catch up. The dangers of debt are always taught to children, but there must be some practical advice given on how to stay out of debt for good. What we have been taught about good debt and bad debt must be completely repackaged. All debt is bad debt. There is no good debt and bad debt theory, it is all bad debt. Now, this where your mindset is challenged. Right now, your thought process is being challenged because this is all new to you. You will tell yourself, *well, I just need one or two credit cards for emergencies, right?* I have to challenge you, dear reader, who told you this? Who taught you this? You also might tell yourself that your credit score is important, but is it really? Your credit score is an indication that you spend a lot of money and, if you give it some more thought, your credit cards that you are carrying around? Well, it's like carrying your bills around with you; it's as if your bills are attached to you. And every time you swipe that card, your debt goes up. You may get a few "points", but that is irrelevant. Be it a black card, gold card or a rewards member, the more debt you carry, the harder it is to come out of it.

Years ago, I heard a story of a man who always took a walk in the neighborhood to get some exercise, and as he took the same route every day, he would always wave to those who were passing by and give smiles to mothers who were with their children walking down the street. But as he passed by this one home, he would always hear a dog moaning and groaning.

This went on for days, with the dog's moaning beginning to get louder, so after days of hearing this dog suffer, the gentleman walked up to the owner and said, "Forgive me for being in your business, but what is wrong with your dog?"

The owner replied, "He is lying on a nail."

"So, he is lying on a nail, you say."

The owner said, "Yes, sir."

So, the man asked, "Why doesn't he just get up?"

The owner answered, "It's not hurting him bad enough to get up."

So, if your debt is hurting you that bad and all you do is moan and groan and complain about the interest rate and moan about not having enough, more than likely, the mindset is locked into being in debt for a very long time. As of November 2021, our current inflation rate is skyrocketing as President Biden has signed a stimulus bill to help build our infrastructure here in the United States. When it comes to the future, America always seems to be lagging behind, playing catch up. What I find hard to believe is that the more taxes Americans pay, the more behind our communities are.

All right, let's think this out. We pay federal tax, income tax property taxes, and each time we vote, there is always an initiative to vote on for funding schools or building better highways, and also to help build better transportation for the next generation.

So, with all of the money being taking out for the future, why is there never a surplus? I don't mind paying taxes, or paying my fair share, but I don't want to do it all by myself. Since we are paying property taxes every year, it would be a breath of fresh air if our taxes went down a few hundred dollars on our land. The message I am conveying to you is that if you live in a small town or a city that has millions, it is very possible that your community is in debt, deep debt. This why our taxes are being raised, but as the price goes higher and workers are barely keeping their heads above water, solutions don't seem to be on the agenda of newly elected officials.

What is needed today more than managers, more than politicians, more than another unkept promise, is leadership. We all can be trained to follow a job description, but what is needed is leadership skill that will actually make a change in the neighborhoods that we live in.

Because, if there is household debt in the neighborhood, there is community debt, and if the block you live on has every person in debt, how can we help others?

Once again, let me throw up a disclaimer. Yes, I do understand that life will bring circumstances beyond our control, so this book is in no way finger pointing, but rather trying to get you to think about the dangers of being in debt long term. Debt kills dreams, and it does it by the generations.

Now, let me go off script for a moment. One of reasons that most Americans are behind the eight ball when it comes to finances has to do with education, or the lack thereof, and also not knowing the right people. We, as a people, have known for quite some time that African Americans are over four-hundred years behind when it comes to our economic growth. Believe it or not, there was some growth for African Americans when John Alvord opened the Freedman's bank in 1865, with assets over three-million dollars and thirty-seven branches open in seventeen states. It was vital for the black families after President Lincoln freed slaves, but little attention was given to the law that was signed into act which President Lincoln had a part in making sure the Freedman's bank was open. This part of history is not often talked about, because the focus was on the forty acres and a mule which was promised to the families of slaves. Now, with land and money to put in a bank, families' futures were looked promising, but after seven years, the bank closed due to mismanagement. Pioneer Frederick Douglass was called in to be the president, but it was too little, too late. What happens when you don't have the right tools? The right team members? The result is mismanagement and playing catch-up, and this is what most workers are doing right now in the United States, playing catch-up, working two jobs, putting in sixteen hour days, all while trying to balance a home life for their families.

When a person is free from debt, their mindset changes, their whole world comes into focus and they realize they can never go back to how it was. Growth is hard for some people because it presents a challenge. You will be surprised how your friends and family will turn on you when you start to grow, and once you grow, your attitude changes. You desire more on the other side of life. Financial literacy will open doors for you and your great-grandchildren, but the process must begin immediately, before the world realizes they are unprepared for the future.

Have you ever forgotten important documents?

Ignored company emails that could have made your job better? Decided to postpone that parent-teacher conference?

Put off home repairs until a later date? If you answered yes to any of these questions, it is quite possible you are walking into your future unprepared, and when you are not prepared, your children know it. Oh, they cannot express it or articulate what they observe; however, they do see the anguish on your face and the question marks in your eyes. The time is now. You must respond to your responsibility.

Chapter 8

Generational Mindset

The hardest thing for a man, woman, teenager or a senior citizen to do, is to change the way they think. Breaking with tradition, is a monster; the mind has become so accustomed to being repetitive, if it hears change coming through the ear canals, the brain will put on brakes and say, "Wait just a minute here. Who approved this new itinerary?" Change is hard for a lot of people, and there are others who say, "Bring it on!" Fear is the Achilles' heel of our future. We believe if we hide long enough that the responsibility will just go away, and meanwhile, our children are growing up without a blueprint or a guide on how to navigate life when it becomes too much to handle.

Perhaps you are familiar with the phrase, 'Stay out of my business', or 'Mind your beeswax', or the most popular phrase for the 21st century, 'Why you all up in my business? Get your own business!' The sad truth behind all of these statements is nobody wants anyone in their business until they need help. It is understandable how in today's society, where there is so much content creation on social media, Instagram, Facebook (a.k.a.) Metaverse and YouTube, every life now seems to be an open book.

But there is the small part of everyone's life that is guarded and under lock and key. Why is that?

Financial education is a foreign language to many of us because this was not passed down in our family tree, so what we have are really good memories of the past but no blueprint for the future.

Planning for the future takes the burden off households who have lost their loved ones. If there is no plan, then the future is uncertain. I was surprised to read articles of high-profile celebrities and dignitaries who died without a will or any estate planning. Dr. Martin Luther King, who led the civil rights movement, died with no will in place, and up to the year 2012, the family of Dr. King and his friends had not settled their dispute. The queen of soul, Aretha Franklin, died without a will. R&B legend Prince? No will. Singer and R&B artist Barry White, no will. Grunge performer Kurt Cobain, worth multi-millions, did not have a will. Jimi Hendrix and President Abraham Lincoln all passed away with no plan in place.

So, what happens when there are no instructions? Well, in that case, the state and the courts decide your family's future, and when that happens, you and your family are at the mercy of the courts. In my first book, I mentioned how Terri and I were sued seven times in three years. This happened even with a will in place. Just because you have a will, does not mean it cannot be challenged by a member of the family. It's still best to have a plan in place for you and your family. In order to have the right mindset, you must change your behavior, and also revaluate who is giving you information, because we are living in a day and time where one size fits all does not fit any more. You don't have to cut off people from your life, but you may want to add others who will be beneficial in helping you to succeed. I have a coworker who always tells me this. "George!" he would say with a thunderous voice from the back of kitchen. "I was asking why is it taking so long for the food to come out to the front?"

Son Ha would always answer, "Good food takes time."

Success? Yes, success takes time, relearning takes time. Ask yourself why you are working so hard? What is your reason to get up in the morning? When your shift is over at work, did you make a difference in someone else's life?

The American workers need to go back to basics

so they can excel to the point where their mind

is not always full of questions about their future.

Let's go over a few mindset laws that should

help us all think.

Mindset law (1) You do not have to work on a

job until you are sixty-five or seventy.

Put a plan in place now and find the "right"

financial planner. Mindset law (2) You do not

need credit to build wealth; your credit score

does not indicate if you are wealthy, it just opens

up more ways for you to spend money, and that

leads you right back into debt. Mindset law (3)

It would be a wise choice to make if you were to

start teaching your children now about wealth. Start at their age level, reteach, to make sure they understand what they are learning. Remember, once your child is in the 12th grade, they are already twelve years behind. Mindset law (4) Make sure you have your estate planning in order.

Let me revisit why wills and estate planning are important. Three years ago, actor Chadwick Boseman had a breakout role in the blockbuster movie, Black Panther. The movie was such a success that Boseman signed up for the sequel. Sadly, as the sequel was set to start filming, Chadwick Boseman passed away, also without having a will in place. Estate planning is not just for the wealthy. Mindset law (5) Insurance policies are a must for every family. Keep in mind, GoFundMe is not a plan for your future. While I do understand the purpose behind GoFundMe, long term, this is not helpful for your future. Mindset law (6) Get out of debt now! Let me say this again, get out of debt now! Why? Because the debt you are piling up will eventually fall into the lap of your family. Remember, being debt free brings much more clarity to your life. Also remember, before you sign up for any online real estate class, before you click the link in the bio of any YouTuber or a finance celebrity on Instagram, what you are seeing is a very polished presentation of what the content creator wants you to see. Also know that the majority of these social media content creators do not have a M.B.A. in business and quite possibly are carrying a lot of debt. I do realize the times are different, but we all must be careful of whom we let have access to our ear gate, because if you click the link and sign up and swipe that card, there is no going back; you will need sound advice when it comes to your financial future.

Mindset law (7) Prepare now for your tomorrow. In the last few months, we all have been hearing of the word hyperinflation. Basically, It has to do with the dollar losing its value, and because of this, retail store owners are raising their prices, trying to keep up with demand in the retail sector. What draws our attention away from our goals is simple. We become distracted, upset and surprised when we find out how systems work, and what really sets us off is when we realize some employers have been dishonest in presenting how much they can give their employees for raises over the next three years.

Let's look at this more closely. Some employers will offer a three percent raise over the next three years and call this generous, but keep in mind the hyperinflation during that three-year period; the cost of living is going at a higher rate during this time. So, if you get a three percent raise over three years, but the cost of living is going up five percent a year, your three percent is not even meeting the requirements of what it takes to keep up with life's daily routines. So, what can be done? How about hyper-focusing? This can be done by shifting your mindset on your goals. This is how the wealthy stay on top of things. We have to face facts. The majority of workers in the United States of America are severely underpaid and cannot keep up with the cost of living. They seem to be trapped by a system that is not meant to take care of their

employees

So, instead of demands for better wages, take

what they give you and make it work for you.

Yes, gasoline is high, food prices are going

through the roof, and rent and mortgages seem

to have no end as their rates continue to climb.

Once again, let me park here for a moment. I am

not letting big corporations off the hook,

because someone most hold them liable for

how they treat their employees. What we have

to realize is that the more fighting you do, the

more minutes are ticking off the clock, and

before you know it, you are seventy-two years

old with no savings or retirement, and all you have to show for all your hard work is just your opinion.

How about this? The main argument or gripes that employees have is that they want a seat at the table, a voice in the boardroom and for their ideas to be heard. The only way for that to happen is that you must build your own table, your own platform. Corporations do not listen to the little guys; they will bobble their heads and say, "Yes, we hear you," but your concerns will make it no farther. You must build your own future. By doing that, you can take the worry off of your mind and the minds of your family. Don't worry about how you have been treated. Start building; don't clutter your mind with useless, but rather be informed with information that will catapult your future into next level thinking. Surround yourself with others who are likeminded when it comes to finance and retirement. The overall goal is financial freedom, and also to help out to those who are less fortunate. The mindset laws you have been reading are not just so you can get a bunch of toys, because if we really think about it, this is why households are in trouble. They have too many gadgets and toys but no financial peace.

Our whole retirement system needs to be restructured, and the conversation for reparation for African American families now must be put before the senate for a vote. Remember, wounds don't heal until they get addressed.

Mindset law (8) As individuals, you must find your purpose for your life and your future. We also must remember that we will have to carry others to the finish line; we can't just let other people die where they are. In fact, you will realize that others have fallen by the way side. If they are honest with themselves and with you, they will let you know that it's their fault and it's their choices that have gotten them to this place in life. We cannot leave men and women to die on their own. We must make an attempt to help out those who are in need. No, you cannot do it on your own; it will take a village and then some, to help people get back on their feet.

We also have too many cooks in the kitchen, too many financial books that don't have any substantial answers. Too many Instagram posts of people showing off their toys but not a lot of content on what is important, no definitive plan showing how to get out of debt. A debt that is owed will always have a yoke around your future until it is paid in full. What is needed for our young people today is clarity, a plan that will

ensure that no matter what type of economics

or financial depression comes their way, a plan

in place equals a future that cannot be

interrupted.

A flat tire is an interruption. Need a new

transmission? Interruption. No emergency fund

means no plan in place, but if you look around

your home or in your closet, you can see where

your money has gone. Have an iPhone 13

($1,000), maybe three designer bags ($5,000).

Maybe just a few pair of Nikes or Jordans?

$1,000 worth of sneakers? You have a Starbucks

rewards card, right? I know you feel like I am

picking on you. Well, I am not. I just want to get you to think about how the lack of resources are actually right in your own home. You can buy any of these brand name items if you would like, but let's do it this way. Why not invest in Nike, by buying stock in the company? How about investing in Starbucks, let's say a hundred shares, just to start off for a small investment. You might also want to think about McDonald's as an investment. However, when you think about these companies, such as Starbucks and McDonald's, you might also want to think about it this way. It's not just lattes and cappuccinos, it's the land it sits on. Starbucks owns a lot of real estate.

When you think of McDonald's, you don't think of real estate, you think of fast food, but like Starbucks, McDonald's holds multi-millions of dollars in real estate. It's more than fast food. You can buy anything you want, but ask yourself this question, "Who am I making rich?" This is a tough chapter, but hopefully, this will make you realize that you must act now, because if you don't plan your future now, someone else will plan it for you.

These mindset laws? It should change your behavior, make you think. If you are on a 9 to 5 job, you are at the mercy of the employer. Let's do a check list. Your name tag, your office, desk access, parking badge, even your uniform, none of these items belong to you. And what's more shocking is that employees are in shock and in denial when their jobs are eliminated. Their mindset is, "How could they do this to me?" Well, the answer to that question is easy. They do it because they can. They do it because no one holds them accountable.

Mindset law (9) Wake Up. Take these mindset laws and rethink your financial future. Your family is depending on you. You may not be able to take on the banking industry, but you can learn from them and how they make their money. Search out the analytical thinkers, people with character and integrity who will be willing to help you. Lay out a budget plan for your expenses, put away at least months of savings, for emergency fund or what I call J.I.C. (just in case). Make sure you are putting away fifteen percent of your income into a 401k plan at your job. If this sounds like outdated information, believe me, it's relevant and could very well save you from a shipwreck. If you are going to Starbucks five days a week, you might as well buy shares in the company. Have an iPhone? Purchase more than one iPhone? You might want to consider buying stock in the company. At the time of writing this book, Apple stock is at $165 a share, on Tuesday, November 30, 2021. What will it be one year from now? Do not take out a line of credit on your home if you can avoid it. This will put in quicksand. Now, I know that it sounds pretty hard, and like all families, you will want to go on vacations and do what families do together, go to weddings and other activities that bring everyone closer together. Also, make sure to invest in yourself, because if you are not healthy, your future is not healthy.

Reflection

_____

_____

_____

_____

_____

_____

_____

_____

_____

_____

_____

_____

_____

_____

_____

_____

_____

_____

_____

_____

_____

Chapter 9

Remember What Is Really Important

I could not end this book without focusing on what really matters. Your financial education is crucial to your success, but on your journey to the top, be careful how you treat others, make sure you have an anchor that holds your character in place.

Do not let material things and a million dollars allow you believe that this makes you immune from the problems of life. Over two years ago, I was at a stoplight heading towards a hospital for a doctor's appointment, as the crosswalk light came on. I rushed across the street. I thought maybe I was seeing things, forgetting about my appointment as I was walking toward a group of men to get a closer look, because I knew the face I was looking at. I have seen this face on TV and saw him on 60 Minutes. I actually froze for about thirty seconds because I was in disbelief. There he was, larger than life. It was billionaire Paul Allen, owner of the Seattle Seahawks and the Portland Trailblazers. I could not believe it. I watched his team carefully put him into a black Mercedes-Benz, and as the door was shut, the car slowly came to the corner where I was. The traffic light turned red and the crosswalk signal was blinking, allowing me to cross the street, but

I was still. I saw Mr. Allen's face lean into the window of car as his glasses slid slowly away from his face. So, what was he thinking? I have no idea. But I guarantee you, his mind was not on his money. Worth twenty-eight-billion dollars, but his health was failing, and I am sure the medical staff did all they could to save his life. Dear reader, take note and remember your soul is important, your children are priceless. Your word is your bond; don't let any amount of wealth or success contaminate your values or your morals. Don't use your socioeconomic status to put others down. Remember, just because your name is not the hot topic on social media, does not mean there is no legacy. Paul Allen left a legacy that will leave an impact on millions of people. He did good works, along with Microsoft cofounder Bill Gates.

So, what will your legacy be? Whose life is better because of your choices?

When you put this book down, pick up your future and start planning your life.

Blessings to all who have read this book. Remember, someone depends on your success.

As this year is quickly coming to a close, there have been two banks that have closed in California. The interest rate is now 8 percent, and the federal reserve is flirting with raising the interest rate another half percent.

We also must realize that our wealth must have a purpose, a platform. When you give of your time, talent and wealth, life has a way of returning dividends that can be generational. Your wealth needs an assignment. The homeless population across the United States is rising by the day, why? Because no one seems to be fighting poverty. We are fighting wars; we fight with family members, and even your coworkers fight over things that really don't matter. Why? Who's fighting poverty? Over the past six years, Terri and I have been blessed to reach out to the homeless community, feeding over ten thousand people. We have heard stories that would bring tears to your heart. A gentleman told me, "Sir, I never thought I would be in the streets. This is my fault, sir!!" It's so hard to pass judgment on a man who's hungry.

What do you want your legacy to be? Who's depending on you? Are you planning for tomorrow, or are you planning for the next twenty years? What is important is the wellbeing of your family, your integrity and your character. No dollar amount is more important than a person's soul. No dollar amount can buy honesty. Leaving a will for your family is smart, leaving insurance is a must. But leaving a legacy for your family goes far beyond any dollar value.

How awesome would it be, knowing that a father has been there for his family, or a mother has passed down morals and wisdom to her daughter?

Money, for most people, is a hard conversation. It's not talked about until you have to talk about it. It uneasy because of guilt; it's hard because we realize we didn't know what to do. Some people are embarrassed because they feel it's too late to be debt free. Remember, it's never too late for financial freedom. And what does financial freedom mean to you? Well, it gives you back your freedom and your time. In the book of Ecclesiastes, the Solomon writer has brilliant insight to financial matters as he says "money answers all things ". But if we look at things a little closer Solomon looked at all the wealth he had accumulated and referred to it as vanity. It did nothing for his soul it vexed his spirit. In the year 2023 King Solomon would be worth over 3 trillion dollars what a massive amount of wealth, but what is important? I will let you decide. Yes, money answers all things but in the end that is all it is, things, material things that only last momentarily remember everything has a time stamp on it. So, as you go forth on your path to financial freedom remember to keep character in front of your windshield and your past in your rearview mirror.